the EAGLE

America's Inspiration

the EAGLE

America's Inspiration

Photographs by Jack A. Barrie
Text by Gerhard Gschwandtner

Personal Selling Power, Inc., Fredericksburg, Virginia

The Eagle, America's Inspiration
Text Copyright © 1996 by Gerhard Gschwandtner
Photographs Copyright © 1996 by Jack A. Barrie

The Eagle, America's Inspiration is published in the United States
by Personal Selling Power, Inc., P.O. Box 5467,
Fredericksburg, VA 22403. Tel. 540/752-7000.

Permissions acknowledgments:
On page 119:
Anheuser-Bush logo provided courtesy of Anheuser-Bush Companies, Inc.
Philadelphia Eagles logo provided courtesy of Philadelphia Eagles Football Club,
permission to use the logo courtesy NFL Properties, Inc.
Jeep Eagle logo provided courtesy Jeep/Eagle Division of Chrysler Corporation
United States Postal Service logo provided courtesy United States Postal Service
On page 123:
Eagle mask Copyright by Lyle Wilson. Photograph by Kenji Nagai. Photo
courtesy the Inuit Gallery of Vancouver, Ltd.

Design: Beth Ashton, Jennifer Linch, and Marc Oxborrow

Library of Congress Catalog Card#: 96-70216

ISBN# 0-939613-09-3

Acknowledgments

No major creation springs from a void. This book is the result of a team effort from the staff of SELLING POWER magazine. Special thanks go to the design team – Beth Ashton and Jennifer Linch with intern Shadi Ardalan, supervised by art director Marc Oxborrow. Laurie Ross and Dana Ray proof read countless generations of text.

Laura Gschwandtner's firm hand moved the production ahead of schedule (yes, we created the book from start to finish in under five hectic, but thrilling months). Laura also produced a videotaped progress report for Jack Barrie. We are grateful to Jack's friend Wayne Campbell, one of the leading ornithologists in North America (and author of 40 books), for taking time to review and validate the eagle facts in this book. And a special note of thanks to Walter Sovde who took Jack Barrie and me by boat to some of the most thrilling eagle watching I could imagine.

I would like to express my personal thanks to the staff of SELLING POWER for creating enough free time in my schedule to turn this book idea into reality. A special tribute goes to Stella Barrie. We dedicate this book to her.

Contents

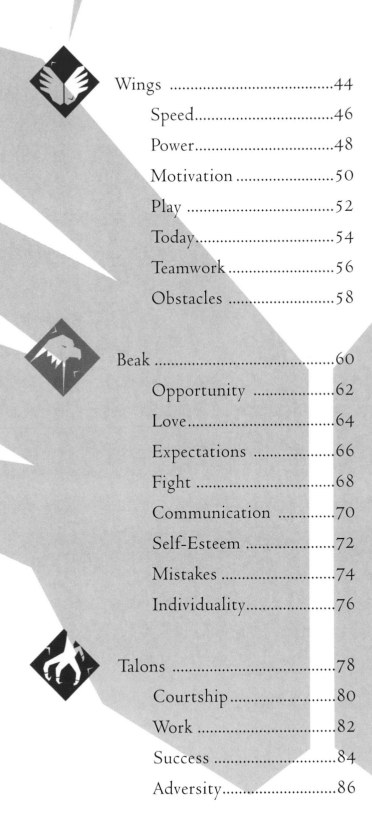

Foreword

Few Americans have ever seen a Bald Eagle in the wild gracefully soaring overhead against an azure sky. Because there are relatively few eagles living among us, we tend to forget the original reasons the founding fathers chose it over all other creatures as the symbol of a nation — reasons that still hold — grace, intelligence, speed, accuracy, beauty and, above all, power.

I saw my first Bald Eagle at dawn from the deck of a sailboat. In fact two eagles were walking on an island beach about a quarter of a mile from where we were anchored. One look through field glasses and I was astonished not only by their size, but also by their grandeur. At that moment my love for eagles began.

The idea for this book began years later when I bought a magazine with a dramatic cover picture of a Bald Eagle taken by Jack Barrie. I was so moved by his breathtaking photography that I felt compelled to call him. I discovered that in the 15 years since retiring from the Royal Canadian Mounted Police, Jack had taken more than 20,000 photographs of Bald Eagles. To get the best possible shots, he had built special equipment and worked constantly at improving his techniques. Jack's work has been featured on the covers of hundreds of magazines and in several books.

When I described a book combining interesting eagle facts and motivational quotes with his pictures, Jack said that he liked the idea. A week later Jack sent us 200 slides — a small sample of his best work. The pictures were perfection. Two weeks later, I was in Jack's home looking at 20,000 of the most incredible slides I had ever seen.

One day we went on a boat ride to visit a number of eagles' nests. At one point Jack tossed a herring overboard. Within seconds, one of the eagles swooped down from the trees, quickly grabbed the fish and returned to its perch. Although I had my camera ready, all I could capture was the reflection of the Bald Eagle on the water's surface. (See picture right.) Jack

Barrie is the sole photographer of all Bald Eagle images in this book. My hat's off to him and to the reader who joins us in this journey aloft.

Introduction

The eagle has captured human imagination for centuries. The ancient Greeks believed in the power of Zeus, the god of the sky. He used an eagle as his messenger. Ancient Romans carried eagle statues on a flagpole as a symbol of military power. European rulers have used the image of the eagle on their coats of arms. In 1155, Frederick Barbarossa, the King of the Romans, chose the double-headed eagle as the symbol of power of the Holy Roman Empire.

Many birds are larger than the eagle, have wider wingspans and can fly faster, but throughout the world, the eagle still is regarded as the king of the skies among nearly 9,000 species of birds in the world.

North American Indian folklore describes the eagle as a bird of warning. Indian legends speak of the Thunderbird, most powerful of all eagles, capable of creating flashes of lightning with its eyes and thunderclaps with its wings.

Of all eagles, the mature Bald Eagle is the most regal looking, with a dark brown body, dark wings, a white head and 12 white tail feathers. The Bald Eagle lives only in North America. It is estimated that there are a mere 4,700 pairs of Bald Eagles living in the contiguous United States and 20,000 pairs in Alaska.

On June 20, 1782, Congress voted the image of the Bald Eagle for the Great Seal of the United States. At the time of the vote, Benjamin Franklin thought that the turkey had more redeeming features, writing to his daughter:

"I wish the Bald Eagle had not been chosen as a representative of our country. He is a bird of bad moral character; he does not get his living honestly...the turkey is a more respectable bird."

The Bald Eagle has become a source of American pride. When an American president speaks, the image of a Bald Eagle adorns the lectern; when the president's plane takes off, flight controllers refer to the plane as "Eagle One." When Neil Armstrong landed on the moon, Houston control reported, "The eagle has landed."

The image of the Bald Eagle has become an elegant metaphor for truly American qualities: The white head symbolizes wisdom; the large wings suggest the ability to gain perspective and maintain freedom; the sharp, black talons have the power to seize and carry prey, an ability that commands respect and independence; the keen eyesight evokes images of vigilance; the sharp yellow beak gives a royal appearance; and the white tail feathers add to the natural beauty of the proud bird. The Bald Eagle is America's symbolic messenger to the rest of the world, communicating power, independence and strength.

This book looks at the world of the Bald Eagle and reveals its magic and meaning. As Bald Eagles speak to us through inspiring images, we can review the thoughts of inspiring humans who have soared above the crowd.

This is a book for those who have not given up on the dream to soar far beyond everyday life.

eyes

In a side-by-side comparison, the eye of a Bald Eagle is slightly larger than the eye of an adult human. The eagle's eye sockets are set deeply in the skull and the greater distance between the lens and the retina explains why the Bald Eagle exceeds the visual acuity of humans by a factor of three to one. Research shows that Bald Eagles can detect prey the size of a rabbit about a mile away.

To protect the eagle's powerful eyes, a bony brow, called a supraorbital ridge, reduces glare from the sun. In addition, a "third eyelid" called the nictitating membrane covers the eyeball like a greyish film. This transparent membrane brushes over the eye regularly to help prevent injury and keep the eye clean. Eagles have excellent depth perception and can judge distances accurately. For example, when they spot a fish, they know exactly where to place their talons to grab the fish and not its image refracted as seen through the water.

When a Bald Eagle looks out over its territory, it perceives a more colorful world and finer details than the human eye. Since their necks can rotate 200 degrees, two eagles perched facing each other are in complete control of their surroundings.

When an intruder enters the territory of a nesting pair, the eagles begin their attack long before the intruder is aware it has trespassed.

Bald Eagles are sensitive to the magnetic fields of the earth. It is believed that eagles can compare light from the sun with magnetic fields through the nervous system and use the information as a directional compass during migration.

Best time to look for Bald Eagles

Time of the year: In the fall, after the leaves have fallen, eagles become more visible as they congregate near sources of food such as spawning fish and waterbirds.

Time of the day: In the morning, right after sunrise, they tend to be more active, hunting for prey. On a sunny, breezy day, eagles like to soar the skies, riding thermals between 800 and 2,000 feet. On hot summer days, eagles often spend hours perched on a tree, preening, resting and calling to each other. During the last hours before sunset, they tend to resume their feeding activities before retiring to traditional evening roost sites.

14

We all live under the same sky, but we don't all have the same horizon.

KONRAD ADENAUER

Vigilance

*B*ald Eagles have keen eyesight and binocular vision. Once they spot a target, their pupils focus within a few milliseconds. Their sharp eyes are much more powerful than the human eye. Eagles are acutely aware of their surroundings and are able to perceive near-ultraviolet light.

Remember, when the eagle
looks down on the still water, his
reflection is that of a noble bird.
If you choose right over wrong,
the reflection you see will be that
of a noble person.
Our lives mirror the path
each of us chooses to follow.

ROBERT JAMES CHALLENGER

Reflecti

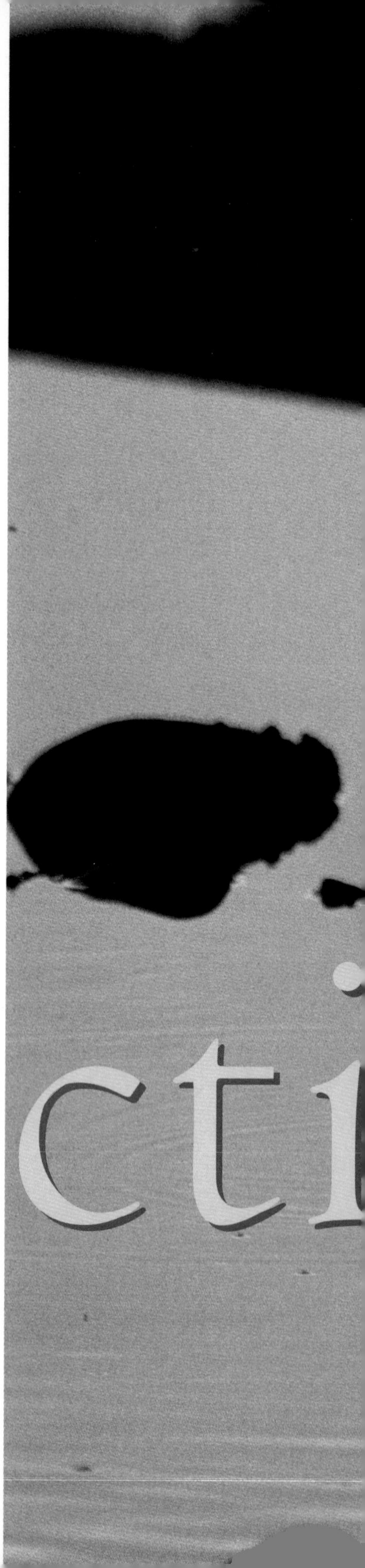

Best equipment for observing eagles

There are two types of equipment you can use for watching Bald Eagles:

1. *Birding Binoculars* A good pair of binoculars will give you about 8X magnification and a good view of a Bald Eagle in action.

2. *Spotting Scope* If you prefer to get the feeling of being really close to the eagle, check out a spotting scope. Built like a telescope, the spotting scope offers you 20X - 60X magnification. This allows you to zoom in to the eagle's eyes, view the details of the feathers or observe the sharp talons. Spotting scopes are about three times more expensive than binoculars and require a tripod or other solid support.

Alaska

Anchorage
Haines
Juneau

America's largest Bald Eagle concentrations

The top ten states:
Estimated number
of breeding pairs

1.	Alaska	20,000
2.	Florida	700
3.	Minnesota	600
4.	Washington	500
5.	Wisconsin	500
6.	Oregon	260
7.	Michigan	260
8.	Maryland	180
9.	Virginia	175
10.	Maine	160

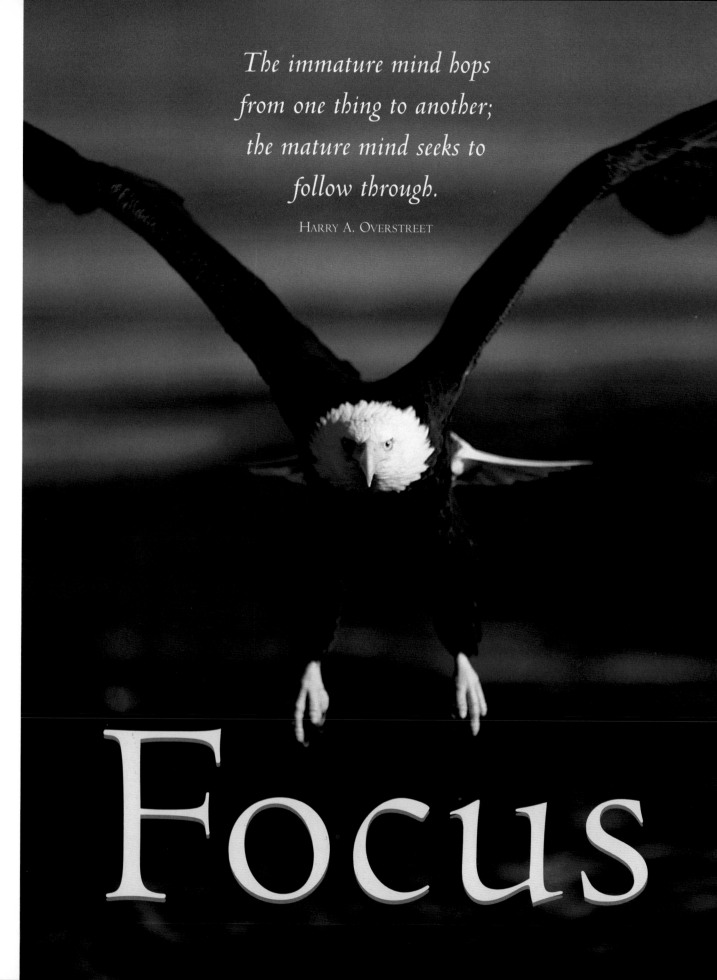

*The immature mind hops
from one thing to another;
the mature mind seeks to
follow through.*

HARRY A. OVERSTREET

FOCUS

*Do today's duty, fight today's temptation;
do not weaken and distract yourself by looking
forward to things you cannot see, and could not
understand if you saw them.*

CHARLES KINGSLEY

*I am not the smartest or most talented person in
the world, but I succeeded because I kept
going, and going, and going.*

SYLVESTER STALLONE

The purpose of life is a life of purpose. ROBERT BYRNE

Goals

The tragedy of life doesn't lie in not reaching your goal. The tragedy lies in having no goal to reach. It isn't a calamity to die with dreams unfulfilled, but it is a calamity not to dream. It is not a disgrace to reach for the stars, but it is a disgrace to have no stars to reach for. Not failure, but low aim, is a sin.

BENJAMIN MAYS

*A man's got to know
his limitations.*

CLINT EASTWOOD

22

Wisdom

'But you never were made, as I,
On the wings of the winds to fly!'
The eagle said.

WILL CARLETON

Oh, if at every
moment of our lives
we could know the
consequences of some
of the utterings,
thoughts and deeds
that seem so trivial
and unimportant
at the time!

And should we not
conclude from such
examples that there
is no such thing in
life as unimportant
moments devoid
of meaning for
the future.

sight

How to photograph Bald Eagles

In the continental United States, most Bald Eagles are very shy and avoid humans. Since the eagle's vision is better than a human's, it will fly away long before the photographer gets a chance to spot it. The pictures in this book are the result of 15 years of patience and hard work. Here are five steps that Jack Barrie recommends for getting good eagle pictures:

1. Explore and observe first. Familiarize yourself with the eagles' territory. Spend time studying their habits. Keep a daily log of the eagles' movements.

2. Determine the best location. Set up a blind in a safe and dry place that gives you a good view of the location where you have spotted eagles before.

eagle
THOUGHT

But they that wait
upon the Lord shall
renew their strength.
They shall mount up
with wings like eagles.
They shall run and
not be weary.
And they shall walk,
and not faint.
ISAIAH 40:31

26

Raptors use body language to communicate with each other and defend their breeding and foraging territory. When an intruder enters the "restricted" zone, the eagle flies above the invader and lowers his legs — talons extended — as a warning sign. All birds know this danger signal and take quick evasive action.

ertness

When young eagles feel threatened, they will extend their wings and raise their heads to appear larger. If that move does not deter the intruder, they will fan their tail and sit on their back with their feet pointed against the enemy and their talons ready to strike.

You can purchase a portable, camouflaged blind in a good sporting goods store. Be prepared to sit for several hours before the eagles return to their perch site. Always respect the eagles' habitat and keep at a safe distance.

3. *Use the best available equipment.* Rent or buy the longest and fastest telephoto lens you can get. To start, you might consider a 300 mm, f 2.8, auto focus lens. Use a 2X teleconverter to boost the performance to 600 mm at f 5.6. To photograph an eagle catching fish you need a motor drive capable of producing six frames per second. Many professionals use 100 ISO slide film. Get a sturdy tripod with a head that allows easy movement in all directions.

*You can't depend
on your eyes when
your imagination
is out of focus.*

MARK TWAIN

Attention

We have to try to cure our faults by attention and not by will.

SIMONE WEIL

4. Practice focusing and framing. To capture a fast-moving eagle with a seven-foot wingspan in a single frame – without cropping parts of the bird – is a major challenge for any photographer. To learn the skill of "panning," Jack Barrie practiced for hours by following cars on a highway, looking through his telephoto lens mounted on a tripod. If your camera has continuous autofocus, be sure to keep the eagle in the center of the frame, otherwise the camera will focus on the sky behind the eagle and you'll end up with a blurred picture. To freeze the motion of your subject and to allow for the rapid movement of your lens, use shutter speeds of 1/500th of a second or faster.

The feathers of the mature Bald Eagle are nothing short of a masterpiece. The long, dark brown body and wing feathers are in sharp contrast to the pure white head and tail, giving the magnificent bird a regal, stunning appearance. Feathers may control flight maneuvers, regulate body temperature, repel water, serve as camouflage, and help attract a

feathers

mate. Eagles shed their feathers and grow new ones every year in a gradual process called molting. Each feather consists of a vertical shaft and hundreds of fine horizontal branches. These "branches," called barbs, are very flexible and separate easily under pressure. For example, if the eagle's wing hits a tree limb, the feathers bend and the branches may separate in several places. The fine branches of the feather are held together by a velcro-like system of very small and flexible barbs that have small hooks at the end. Preening reconnects the separated barbs and rearranges the feathers. Oil taken by the beak from a gland near the base of the tail and spread over the plumage makes the feathers shine and keeps them flexible and water repellent.

Newly born eagle chicks are covered with greyish, fluffy down. During the first year, young eagles molt to black tail feathers that are longer than those of their parents, giving them the appearance of a larger and stronger bird and providing immature eagles with an extra lift to practice their flying skills and hunting abilities. Since their beaks are black and their feathers are blackish brown with a few white streaks, young eagles are well camouflaged when perched in a tree. During successive stages of molting, the Bald Eagle gradually develops its trademark white head, yellow beak and white tail feathers by its fifth year.

Grace

A true work of art is but a shadow of the divine perfection.

MICHELANGELO

Quill Pens

For 1,000 years, mankind relied on the quill pen and ink for writing letters and books. The best pens came from the outer wing feathers of large birds. Left-handed people would prefer the curved feathers from the right wing and right-handed people would use the feathers from the left wing.

During the Middle Ages, monks wrote and copied books using quill pens; as a result, the quill became synonymous with the word of God.

Quill pens made from goose feathers were common; however the upper class used eagle feathers.

Sensitivity

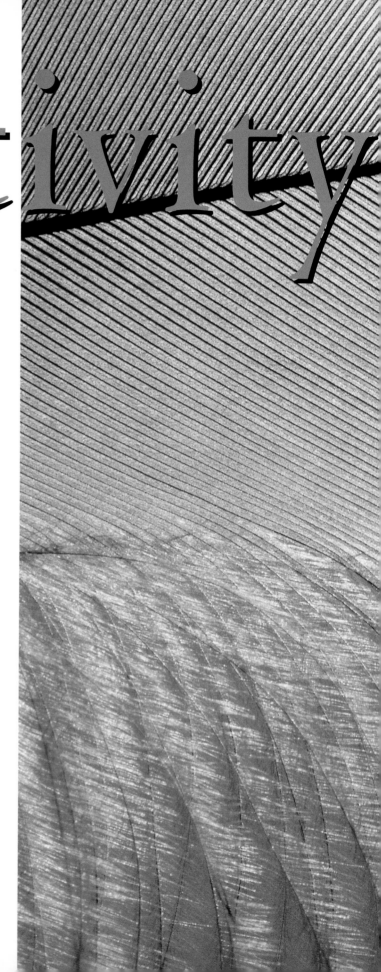

Believe, when you are most unhappy, that there is something for you to do in the world. So long as you can sweeten another's pain, life is not in vain.

HELEN KELLER

Let us permit nature to have her way: She understands her business better than we do.

MICHEL DE MONTAIGNE

34

Attit

ude

One can make a day
of any size, and
regulate the rising and
setting of one's own
sun and the brightness
of its shining.

JOHN MUIR

Flexibility

The survival of the
fittest is the ageless
law of nature, but the
fittest are rarely the
strong. The fittest are
those endowed with
the qualifications for
adaptation, the ability to accept the
inevitable and conform to the
unavoidable, to harmonize with
existing or changing conditions.

DAVE E. SMALLEY

eagle
FACT

Feathers are flexible...
Eagles replace their
feathers annually fol-
lowing a gradual,
symmetrical sequence
over a period of time
that does not cause a
loss in flying abilities.
Bald Eagles begin
molting from the
inner primary feathers
on each wing moving
outward to the
wingtips. The 12 tail
feathers start molting
from the center to the
outer edges.

Whoever has no patience has no wisdom.

ANONYMOUS

*Have patience with all things, but
chiefly have patience with yourself.
Do not lose courage in considering
your own imperfections but instantly
set about remedying them –
every day begin the task anew.*

SAINT FRANCIS DE SALES

Patience

Happiness

The happiness of your life depends
on the quality of your thoughts.

MARCUS AURELIUS

When eaglets grow their first flight feathers (age 10-12 weeks), they intently watch their parents taking off, soaring, and returning to the nest. A Bald Eagle's flying skills are the envy of any pilot. Eagles can hover in place, reverse direction in a split second, fly upside down, roll over from head to tail or

wings

sideways, dive at breakneck speed and perform cartwheels by locking their talons with others of their kind.

The powerful and finely toned muscles of Bald Eagles can control the position of each individual wing and tail feather. The feathers channel the flow of air over, and under, the wings. Eagles adjust their wings and feathers to slow down, to increase lift, to stabilize the pitch, to start a turn, or to reduce turbulence.

Bald Eagles use air efficiently; they only flap their wings if it is absolutely necessary. They take advantage of air currents, wind direction and thermals to rise and soar without great effort. As eagles mature, they learn how to conserve energy and hunt with the least amount of effort. Immature eagles, who are developing the art of flight, often spend hours looking for food and may depend on such carrion as dead fish for nutrition.

When young eagles spread their wings for the first time, a current of air may pass over their feathers, creating a vacuum under the wing. The resulting force will gently lift the startled bird who will quickly fold its wings and drop down into the nest. At first, the eaglets will hop up and down, exercising their wing muscles; then they will manage to fly from one side of the nest to another, then hop out to a branch and fly back to the nest. This process may take as long as a week.

To motivate their offspring to fly, a parent may bring food back to the nest, display it in midair, and continue the flight to a tree near the nest. After a few encouraging calls from the parent, the hungry eaglet will soon move to the edge of the nest, spread its wings and fall forward into flight. Many times the other parent will fly close behind.

Sometimes eaglets misjudge their first landing and crash into a tree, hanging upside down for a few anxious moments, screeching and swinging, until they've regained their balance.

Take your best shot. Go with your full strength and at full speed. Then you won't have to spend the next day thinking of what you should have done and of what might have been.

HOWARD FERGUSON

Speed

The top diving speed of a Bald Eagle can exceed 100 mph. When migrating, eagles cruise at speeds between 35 and 45 mph. The most energy-consuming form of flight is hovering.

Immature eagles invest up to 500 percent more time and energy flying and searching for food than adults. Their flying power and speed is equal to, or better than, the adults', but their hunting abilities are not yet fully developed.

Mankind's dream

To fly like a bird is a
dream that has filled
mankind's consciousness
for thousands of years.
The story of Icarus was
first told more than 2,000
years ago. According to
legend, the Greek architect
Daedalus constructed
wings using feathers
joined by wax. He and his
son Icarus escaped an
island prison by flying
over the sea. Icarus had
strong arms that allowed
him to fly closer to the
sun. The sun's rays melted
his wings and he hurtled
into the sea and drowned.

ICARUS DRAWING COURTESY
OF THE BETTMAN ARCHIVE

*Reach high, for
stars lie hidden
in your soul.
Dream deep, for
every dream
precedes the goal.*
Pamela Vaull Starr

Power

Motivati

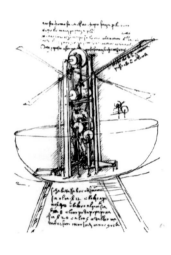

A new vision

In 1499, Leonardo da
Vinci designed the
ornithopter, an airplane
with flappable wings. He
also drew a helicopter and
studied the possibility of
creating a glider plane.

LEONARDO DA VINCI ORNITHOPTER DRAWING
COURTESY OF THE BETTMAN ARCHIVE

on

To be what we are,
and to become what we are
capable of becoming, is the
only end of life.

BARUCH SPINOZA

Reality

In 1899, Orville and Wilbur Wright built their first glider plane, a biplane kite. Studying aerodynamics, the Wright brothers developed wings that could be twisted to control basic flight movements such as climbing, descending and banking. After three years of experimenting with gliders, they built their motorized plane. In December 1903, they flew a short stretch of 852 feet. The entire flight lasted 59 seconds.

Play so that you may be serious.

ANACHARSIS

L ike humans, eagles like to enjoy themselves. Once they have eaten and fed their offspring, one may take a little tidbit of food, like a chunk of seal meat or salmon, and fly away with two or three eagles chasing behind. Sometimes it will drop the meat from about 200 feet and another eagle will swoop underneath and catch it in midair. Then the chase starts all over until the eagle drops the meat and another eagle catches it right before it hits the water.

Play

There are two things to aim for in life: first, to get what you want; and, after that, to enjoy it. Only the wisest achieve the second.

LOGAN PEARSALL SMITH

Today

Success!

The U.S. Space Shuttle weighs 4.5 million lbs. at take-off. Two minutes later it reaches an altitude of 150,000 feet, the zone at which weightlessness occurs, where all humans can fly.

SHUTTLE PHOTO COURTESY OF NASA

*No longer forward
nor behind
I look in hope or fear;
but grateful, take the good
I find the best of
now and here.*

JOHN GREENLEAF WHITTIER

*Yesterday is ashes;
tomorrow wood.
Only today does
the fire burn brightly.*

ESKIMO PROVERB

eagle

FACT

When eagles catch pockets of rising warm air, they can quickly reach altitudes of 2000-3000 feet - without flapping their wings. Given the right weather conditions, Bald Eagles can soar to alltitudes of 10,000 feet.

Eagles don't flock together. You'll find
them one at a time.

ROSS PEROT

Teamwork

*S*uch abundance of food as spawning salmon in the Pacific Northwest and in Alaska attracts feeding flocks of thousands of Bald Eagles. While eagles will vigorously defend their breeding territory, they often form a highly sociable "feeding flock" away from home. The members of the flock enjoy getting large amounts of food with small amounts of effort. The abundance of food reduces aggression and stimulates social interaction.

eagle
FACT

The wingspan of Bald Eagles ranges from 5.5 feet to 8 feet. The smallest Bald Eagles breed in Florida, the largest in Alaska.

The Bird of Washington

On a trip to the Upper Mississippi River, John James Audubon found a large, dark brown eagle with a black beak. Audubon believed that the young eagle was a new species related to the Bald Eagle. Since the Bald Eagle had already been adopted as the emblem of the United States, Audubon thought that the new bird should be named after President George Washington. His idea of the "Bird of Washington" faded quickly after he realized that his new eagle was merely a juvenile Bald Eagle.

Obstacles

The only obstacle to flying more efficiently is the air. Yet, if the air were withdrawn and the eagle were to fly in a vacuum, it would fall instantly to the ground. The very element that offers the resistance to flying is at the same time the condition of flight.

The same principle — that obstacles are conditions of success — holds true in human life. A life free of all obstacles would reduce all possibilities to zero. As eagles overcome the law of gravity by stretching their wings, we can overcome life's obstacles by stretching our abilities.

Obstacles cannot crush me. Every obstacle yields to stern resolve. He who is fixed to a star does not change his mind.

LEONARDO DA VINCI

Bald Eagles are efficient hunters. They tend to go after the most readily available food source that requires the least amount of effort and risk. When hunting live prey, the eagles' favorites are fish and such waterbirds as ducks, geese or herons. Small mammals or such carrion as deer or sea lion are also eaten. Eagles can also kill snakes with one snap of a razor-sharp beak and pluck abalone from rocky seashores. Adult eagles can go several days without food, but to survive, they need to eat food weighing about 10 percent of their body weight each day. During harsh winters they migrate south to find more readily available prey, or visit spawning salmon streams.

Mature eagles weigh between 9 and 14 pounds depending on the season, the food supply and where they live. Females tend to be slightly larger and heavier than the males.

During the breeding period, the male eagle brings food to his mate. After the chicks hatch they are fed beak-to-beak by the female during the first few days. Later, the food is dropped in front of the chicks. To thrive and grow, the nestlings must consume nearly the equivalent of their own weight each day.

The chick that is hatched first tends to have an advantage over its younger siblings. The older and stronger infant will get to the food first and often attack a weaker sibling. If the attacked eaglet is strong enough to defend itself, or fast enough to snatch scraps of food, it will survive.

Sometimes the weaker sibling will create diversions, like playing with a stick, to dis-

beak

tract the rival from the food supply and then steal the meat.

It is common for eagle chicks to push a weaker sibling out of the nest, or to kill it with their sharp talons and eat it when food is scarce. Parents rarely interfere when their offspring are fighting.

The mortality rate for eagles in the first year of life is about 50 percent. The main cause of death is starvation. The mortality rate of the adult Bald Eagle is only 5 percent. The maximum life span of a Bald Eagle is 50 years.

Opportu

*T*he curve of an eagle's beak is designed for tearing meat. The powerful hook helps the eagle expose and prepare food for swallowing. Sawtooth serrations on the roof of the mouth prevent such slippery prey as eels and fish from escaping.

nity

There is no
security on this earth;
there is only opportunity.

DOUGLAS MACARTHUR

A lover's eye will gaze an eagle blind. SHAKESPEARE

Love

*T*he female eagle tears pieces of meat and feeds the chicks individually. When the youngsters are old enough to feed themselves, the parents simply drop the food into the nest.

Expectat

*I long to accomplish
a great and noble task,
but it is my chief duty to
accomplish small tasks as if
they were great and noble.*

HELEN KELLER

*Blessed is he who expects
nothing, for he shall
never be disappointed.*

ALEXANDER POPE

ions

Sometimes it is more important to discover what one cannot do, than what one can do. LIN YUTANG

Fight

The breakfast of champions is not cereal, it's the opposition.

NICK SEITZ

*B*ald Eagles use their voices to communicate a wide range of emotions — bonding, aggression, encouragement, soliciting food, anxiety, or distress. The adults call "kah-kah-kah." Hungry nestlings give a "yaap-yaap-yaap" call. When eagles fight an intruder they will call "ye-ha-ha-ha," with a high-pitched voice. The female eagle's voice has a lower pitch.

Commun

An immature eagle is calling its parent to bring food. Perched in a tree nearby with a fish in its talons, the adult eagle waits for the eaglet to fly.

ication

No one can make you feel
inferior without your consent.

ELEANOR ROOSEVELT

Self-

Human mistakes

The greatest insidious threat to the Bald Eagle's existence arose from the widespread use of DDT and other pesticides after World War II. DDT was sprayed on croplands and its residues washed into lakes and streams. Bald Eagles, and other birds of prey, consumed contaminated fish. The chemicals interfered with the birds' reproductive ability.

eagle
FACT

Nature does not repeat itself. Every eagle has its own individual character, personality and appearance.

Inc.

ividuality

Any power must be the enemy
of mankind which enslaves the
individual by terror and force,
whether it arises under a
Fascist or Communist flag.
All that is valuable in human
society depends upon the
opportunity for development
accorded to the individual.

ALBERT EINSTEIN

Unlike humans, who walk on their foot bones, Bald Eagles walk on their toes. Three toes face forward, one toe points to the rear. This toe arrangement allows the eagle a firm hold while perched in a tree. All four toes are covered with rough pads which also ensure a firm grip on slippery prey. The scales covering the eagle's feet and toes offer protection against snake bites. Each toe is armed with very powerful, curved and pointed talons designed to catch, kill and carry prey.

When an eagle catches a fish, the rear toe, also called the first digit, almost skims the water on the approach, then the eagle spears the fish with its talon and scoops it out of the water, holding it with all toes.

People who handle Bald Eagles in raptor centers or animal hospitals often wear

talons

thick leather gloves (or welders' gloves) to prevent injury from the eagle's sharp and powerful talons.

Without great difficulty, an adult Bald Eagle can carry, and bring back to the nest, prey weighing four pounds. If an eagle catches a larger fish, up to 10 pounds, it may drag the fish across the water using its wings as paddles. What if the eagle catches a larger fish, like say an 18-pound salmon? Wildlife experts have witnessed eagles fight with larger fish for a short time and then drown. Although the eagle can let go of the fish through upward pressure, some eagles get too greedy and won't let go.

The four dagger-like talons are impressive hunting tools. The major hunting methods are:

1. Aerial attack – the Bald Eagle will dive underneath a bird, roll over and strike its talons into the neck or belly to grab it.

2. Piracy – the eagle will pursue birds like osprey or other eagles, and stage a ferocious attack, forcing them to drop their food. The victorious eagle will often dive to catch the falling prey before it hits the ground.

3. Perch and seize – most eagles prefer to wait for prey, like fish, to appear on the water's surface. Then they swoop down with a few powerful strokes of their wings, lower their talons, and lift the victim out of the water.

4. Surveillance flight – a hungry eagle will soar over the foraging zone, sometimes covering three or four miles. As soon as it spots prey, the eagle will go into a high-speed dive that may peak at 100 mph and snatch the prey with one powerful motion, never touching the ground.

When eagles fall in love, they dance in the sky. Eagles often begin their courtship by soaring together, in near perfect synchronized flight. Other courtship rituals include soft calls, mutual preening, and gifts of food offered to the female by its prospective mate. Mating takes place in the nest, or perched on a tree, during a period of about six days before the first egg is laid.

The male eagle dives under the female with his talons stretched out. The female grabs his talons and both begin a free-fall aerial cartwheel roll down to the water. Only inches before impact they separate and return to the skies to continue their dance.

Courtship

Work

Bald Eagles tend to build massive nests in the tallest and strongest trees within sight of water. Skillfully woven of hundreds of sticks interlocked in an impressive structure that can survive fierce storms, an old eagle's nest can weigh more than 4,000 pounds. One nest, in Alaska, was used for more than 70 consecutive years.

Some nests are 20 feet deep and 10 feet wide. It is common for smaller birds such as sparrows, starlings and grackles to build their own nest in the lower parts of an eagle's nest.

Eagles add to and refurbish their nests every year. If the nest is storm-damaged they will build a new nest, usually within a mile of their traditional site.

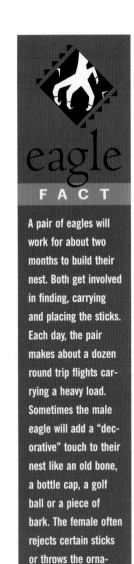

eagle
FACT

A pair of eagles will work for about two months to build their nest. Both get involved in finding, carrying and placing the sticks. Each day, the pair makes about a dozen round trip flights carrying a heavy load. Sometimes the male eagle will add a "decorative" touch to their nest like an old bone, a bottle cap, a golf ball or a piece of bark. The female often rejects certain sticks or throws the ornaments out of the nest.

Far and away the best prize that life offers is the chance to work hard at work worth doing.

THEODORE ROOSEVELT

Success

Theirs is not to reason why,
theirs is but to do or die.

ALFRED, LORD TENNYSON

Adversity

A mature Bald Eagle (top left) steals a scrap of sea lion meat from an immature eagle.

A few seconds later, (bottom left) the immature eagle tries to steal the food back.

Adversity is the diamond dust with which nature polishes its jewels.

SAM ERVIN JR.

By working as a team, seagulls often harass Bald Eagles hoping to get the eagle to share its fish. (above)

Many times eagles simply ignore the small intruders, but when it becomes annoyed the eagle will strike out and kill its enemy.

*There is no failure except
in no longer trying.*

ELBERT HUBBARD

*Success is going from
failure to failure without
loss of enthusiasm.*

SIR WINSTON CHURCHILL

*The important thing is
to learn a lesson
every time you fail.*

RICHARD CUMBERLAND

*Failure is the foundation
of success, and the means
by which it is achieved.*

LAO-TZU

Failure

89

Risk

To achieve anything, you must be prepared to dabble on the boundary of disaster.

STIRLING MOSS

All life is a chance. So take it! The person who goes furthest is the one who is willing to do and dare.

DALE CARNEGIE

Lives of great men all remind us
We can make our lives sublime,
And, departing, leave behind us
Footprints on the sands of time.

HENRY W. LONGFELLOW

Danger

The eagle in the water was struggling with a heavy fish in its talons. The eagle's mate anxiously flew circles over the scene.

The fish pulled the eagle underwater several times, but it kept coming back to the surface. The mate called from midair as if trying to encourage the eagle to persevere. Finally, after a frantic series of wingbeats, the eagle lifted off from the water, its claws free from its deadly grip. After a short flight to shore, the eagle sat for a long time, dripping wet, exhausted and hungry, but alive.

Endangered eagles

The U.S. Fish and Wildlife Service has placed the Bald Eagle on the list of birds in the lower 48 states that are threatened with extinction. While it has staged an encouraging comeback during the past several decades, other eagle species in the world are facing extinction.

Today three of the world's rarest eagles are:

Spanish Eagle:

110 pairs

Madagascar Fish Eagle:

100 pairs

Philippine Eagle:

63 pairs

Some experts believe that birds evolved from theropod dinosaurs. An impression of a bird feather in limestone that formed in the late Jurassic period 160 million years ago suggests a connection between birds and reptiles. The feathers, and the scaled legs of a Bald Eagle, suggest a connection with reptilian scales. The fossil *Archaeopteryx*, indisputably a bird, had anatomical features that were part avian and part reptilian. It had hollow bones, feathers and small teeth, but no big breast bone to support the wing muscles. Researchers believe that this "flying reptile" could fly short distances and had strongly curved opposing toes for grasping like an eagle.

The Bald Eagle occurs only in North America. When European settlers first arrived on our shores, Bald Eagles were a common sight anywhere near water across the nation. Estimates from the 17th century range from 250,000 to 500,000 Bald Eagles on the continent. With the expansion and development of the United States, eagle populations began to decline. Wildlife experts believe that there may have been as many as 75,000 nesting pairs in the lower 48 states when the Bald Eagle was adopted as America's national symbol in 1782. In Alaska, however, Bald Eagles were thriving to the point that local government set a bounty for eagles in 1917. This law was rescinded in 1957.

After World War II, the use of the pesticide DDT for spraying wetland (to control mosquitos) started a steady decline of the species. Bald Eagles ingested contaminated fish and birds and the chemical caused thinning of the egg shells which resulted in reproductive failure. In 1963, a National Audubon Society survey revealed only 417 active eagles' nests in the lower 48 states. In 1967, the Bald Eagle south of the 40th parallel received protection under the Endangered Species Preservation Act. In 1972, DDT was banned from use in the United States and an extensive recovery program

skeleton

began. Wildlife biologists focused on habitat protection, captive rearing, and reintroduction to the wild.

For example, in 1976 there was only one nesting pair of Bald Eagles in the entire state of New York (Finger Lakes Region). The United States Fish and Wildlife Service's Patuxent Research Center, in Maryland, allowed the eagles to incubate their own egg for three weeks, then they removed the egg and replaced it with an eaglet raised in captivity. The eaglet survived and became the first young to fledge in New York State in five years. In a subsequent project, Alaskan eaglets, six to eight weeks old, were flown to the Oak Orchard Wildlife Management Area in western New York, nursed, tagged and released in the Adirondacks. The intensive efforts have slowly increased the state's eagle population to 20 nesting pairs in 1993. Given the success of the nationwide recovery program, in 1995 the U.S. Fish and Wildlife Service reclassified the Bald Eagle from "endangered" to the less critical category of "threatened" throughout the lower 48 states.

95

Vulner

96

ability

We travel together, passengers on a little space ship, dependent on its vulnerable reserves of air and soil; all committed for our safety to its security and peace; preserved from annihilation only by the care, the work, and the love we give our fragile craft.

ADLAI E. STEVENSON

Survival

So much I do love wandering,
so much I love the sea and sky,
That it will be a piteous thing
in one small grave to lie.

ZOË AKINS

Human threats

1. Loss of habitat. Most eagle nests are built in tall trees close to the water's edge. The destruction or degradation of this habitat is one of the greatest threats to the species.

2. Environmental contamination. During the past 15 years the National Wildlife Health Research Center has found more than 100 cases of pesticide poisonings and 225 cases of lead poisoning (lead shot ingested from feeding on dead and dying waterfowl). In addition researchers found high levels of PCB in Bald Eagle eggs in the Midwest, the Northeast and Pacific Northwest.

EAGLE NEST PHOTO BY WAYNE CAMPBELL

Nature has made up her mind that what cannot defend itself shall not be defended.

R.W. EMERSON

Never grow a wishbone
where your backbone
ought to be.

ANONYMOUS

Consi

stency

3. *Hunting.* Although the Bald Eagle is on the threatened species list, some people hunt and kill eagles for fun or out of revenge for stealing small farm animals. During a five year period from 1985 to 1990, the National Wildlife Health Research Center has diagnosed over 150 Bald Eagle deaths due to gunshots.

4. *Human disturbance.* Humans often disturb Bald Eagles during the critical period of courtship, nest building, incubation and brooding. The noise and activity from power boats, jet skis, chain saws or other machinery may flush adults from their nests for an extended time exposing the eggs or eaglets to mortal danger.

The natural world is
dynamic. From the
expanding universe to
the hair on a baby's
head, nothing is the
same from now to the
next moment.

HELEN HOOVER

immature

juvenile

Transfo

subadult

adult

*Nothing maintains
its bloom forever;
age succeeds to age.*

CICERO

rmation

*The more
things change,
the more they
stay the same.*

FRENCH PROVERB

Change

The mind is never satisfied with the objects immediately before it, but is always breaking away from the present moment, and losing itself in schemes of future felicity...

The natural flights of the human mind are not from pleasure to pleasure, but from hope to hope.

SAMUEL JOHNSON

Progress

Mankind is full of tremendously deadly armament, and it has not progressed morally as much as it has scientifically and technically.

Pope Paul VI

Number of Bald Eagle pairs in lower 48 states

Because the Bald Eagle continues to make an astonishing comeback, Americans in great numbers can once again see this graceful, elegant and powerful bird soaring overhead.

4712

3020

1757

791

417

1963   1974   1984   1990   1995

Source: U.S. Fish and Wildlife Service

the American Eagle

The image of the white-headed eagle is an enthusiastic expression of America's ideals. Our forefathers adopted the Bald Eagle as a symbol of freedom, independence and power. In 1782 Charles Thomson, secretary of Congress, developed the first rendering of the Great Seal of the United States. Over time, the Great Seal, with its proud eagle, has been redesigned and improved. Today, the Great Seal is printed on the back of every one dollar bill. In its left talon, the eagle holds 13 arrows - a symbol for war - one arrow for each original colony. In its right talon, the eagle carries an olive branch with 13 leaves - the symbol for peace. The eagle looks toward the olive branch, communicating America's preference for peace.

The eagle is a powerful image that has captured the imagination of every new generation of Americans. To the immigrant, it has become a sign of welcome; to those who serve their country, a symbol of pride; and to all who work on the frontiers of progress, a sign of encouragement.

The Bald Eagle has been adopted as a symbol by the military, the post office and many branches of the U.S. government. Eagle statues grace America's bridges, courthouses, flagpoles and government buildings.

All across the country, communities have chosen the word "eagle" in connection with their towns, lakes, mountains and rivers, including Eagle City, OK; Eagle Falls, NY; Eagle Mountain, CA; Eagle River, AK; Eagle Pass, TX; Eagle Lake, FL; Eagle Grove, IA; Eagle Point, OR; Eagle Rock, NC, and many more.

America's proud history proves that only the strong can be free and to remain strong we must be vigilant, innovative and productive. No nation can survive without powerful symbols and high ideals. Calvin Coolidge once said that "there is no force so democratic as the force of an ideal." America's image is forever linked to the Bald Eagle, the majestic bird that the entire world looks up to. As William Blake wrote in 1790, "When thou seest an eagle, thou seest a portion of genius; lift up thy head."

Pride

In matters of principle,
stand like a rock;
in matters of taste,
swim with the current.

THOMAS JEFFERSON

America

When God made the oyster he
guaranteed his absolute economic and
social security. He built the oyster a
house, his shell, to protect him
from his enemies...
But when God made the eagle,
He declared, "The blue sky is the limit
— build your own house!"
The eagle, not the oyster,
is the emblem of America.

ANONYMOUS

Freedom

*For what avail
the plough or sail,
or land or life,
if freedom fail?*

RALPH WALDO EMERSON

THESE WORDS ARE INSCRIBED ON A PLAQUE IN THE
STAIRWELL OF THE PEDESTAL OF THE STATUE OF LIBERTY.

Eagle One

*When you get to be President,
there are all those things, the honors,
the twenty-one gun salutes...
You have to remember it isn't for
you. It's for the Presidency.*

HARRY TRUMAN

116

This country, with its institutions, belongs to the people who inhabit it. Whenever they shall grow weary of the existing government, they can exercise their constitutional right of amending it, or their revolutionary right to dismember or overthrow it.

ABRAHAM LINCOLN, 1861

No democracy can long survive which does not accept as fundamental to its very existence the recognition of the rights of minorities.

FRANKLIN D. ROOSEVELT, 1938

As the happiness of the people is the sole end of government, so the consent of the people is the only foundation of it.

JOHN ADAMS, 1774

I know no safe depository of the ultimate powers of the society but the people themselves; and if we think them not enlightened enough to exercise their control with a wholesome discretion, the remedy is not to take it from them, but to inform their discretion by education.

THOMAS JEFFERSON, 1820

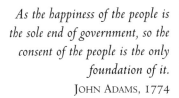

Whenever you have an efficient government you have a dictatorship.

HARRY TRUMAN, 1959

The history of liberty is a history of limitations of government power, not the increase of it.

WOODROW WILSON, 1912

Never before has man had such capacity to control his own environment, to end thirst and hunger, to conquer poverty and disease, to banish illiteracy and massive human misery. We have the power to make this the best generation of mankind in the history of the world - or make it the last.

JOHN F. KENNEDY, 1961

To be prepared for war is one of the most effectual means of preserving peace.

GEORGE WASHINGTON, 1790

Victory

I would say to the House, as I said to those who have joined this Government: "I have nothing to offer but blood, toil, tears and sweat." ...You ask, what is our aim? I can answer in one word: It is victory, victory at all costs, victory in spite of all terror, victory, however long and hard the road may be; for without victory, there is no survival.

WINSTON S. CHURCHILL

Advertising agencies

often use the image of the Bald Eagle as a symbol of power, strength and durability. Companies like Chrysler, American Airlines, Anheuser-Busch, Barclay's Bank, Eagle Electric, Eagle Technology and U.S. Postal Service use the eagle as part of their company logo or their company name. The image of a majestic eagle seems to equate to high quality products or service in the mind of the American consumer.

PHILADELPHIA EAGLES

ANHEUSER-BUSCH COMPANIES

JEEP/EAGLE
DIVISION OF
CHRYSLER
CORPORATION

What a pity is it, that we can die but once to save our country!

JOSEPH ADDISON

Flag of the Office of
the Secretary of the Army

If we desire to avoid insult, we must be able to repel it;
if we desire to secure peace, one of the most powerful instruments
of our rising prosperity, it must be known,
that we are at all times ready for War.

GEORGE WASHINGTON

Loyalty

Always do the job better than the person who gave it to you thought it could be done.

HAL ROBERSON

Character

Genius is formed in quiet,
character in the stream
of human life.
GOETHE

Lyle Wilson

of the Haisla tribe in the Pacific Northwest created this ceremonial eagle mask. Instead of using real eagle feathers, Wilson chose to carve feathers out of yellow cedar saying, "I refused to use real eagle feathers because it would mean the death of an eagle."

Wilson's ancestors were part of the Eagle clan, a group who revered the eagle for its beauty, pride and ferociousness. They believed that the eagle could communicate with the spirits of the sky. Wilson's mask was inspired by the mask of Sunahead, the highest ranking chief of the Eagle clan.

Nature

Thousands of tired, nerve-shaken, over-civilized people are beginning to find out that going to the mountains is going home; that wilderness is a necessity; and that mountain parks and reservations are useful not only as fountains for timber and irrigating rivers, but as fountains of life.

JOHN MUIR

Preferred sites for watching Bald Eagles in the United States

State	Location	Number of Eagles	Time of Year	Contact
Alabama	Lake Guntersville State Park *Eagle tours available in January*	50 - 100	November - February	Lake Guntersville State Park 205/571-5440
Alaska	Chilkat Bald Eagle Preserve	2,500 - 4,000	October - January	Alaska Bald Eagle Festival 907/766-2202 Haines Visitors Bureau 907/766-2234 Alaska State Parks 907-465-4563
Arizona	Mormon Lake	50	November - April	Doug Morrison Overlook on east side of lake
Arkansas	Beaver Lake	180	November - February	Arkansas State Parks 501/682-2187 Winter Wings Festival in Lake Village 501/265-5480
California	Eagle Lake *Best viewing north shore of lake*	40 - 50	November - March	Bureau of Land Management 916/257-0456

State	Location	Number of Eagles	Time of Year	Contact
Colorado	Jackson Lake State Park	100	March, April, May	Jackson Lake State Park 970/645-2551
Florida	Center of Birds of Prey, Maitland *Special Eagle Watch program*	10 - 14	All year	Center of Birds of Prey 407/644-0190
Illinois	Quad Cities - along the Mississippi River	70 - 80	December - February	Quad Cities Visitors Bureau 800-747-7800 Quad Cities Bald Eagle Days (January) 309/788-5912
Iowa	Keokuk Riverfront Area (Mississippi) *Best site at Lock and Dam 19*	300 - 400	November - March	Keokuk Area Tourism Bureau 800-383-1219
Maryland	Blackwater National Wildlife Refuge *Self-guided tours and special viewing area*	50 - 60	All year	U.S. Fish and Wildlife Service 410/228-2677
Minnesota	Chippewa River and Mississippi River Junction Wabasha *Winona sponsors an Eagle Watch program; call 507/452-2272*	70 - 100	November - March	Wabasha Chamber of Commerce 612/565-4158
Montana	Hauser Lake	300	November - December	Helena Chamber of Commerce 406/475-3319
Oregon	Bear Valley National Wildlife Refuge *Klamath Falls sponsors a Bald Eagle Conference. Contact 503/883-5732*	over 500	Mid-November - February	U.S. Fish and Wildlife Service 916/667-2231
Tennessee	Reelfoot Lake *Eagle tours start in January*	200	Late November - early March	Reelfoot Lake State Park 901/253-7756
Texas	Lake Fork Reservoir *Emory sponsors an eagle festival in January*	60	November - March	903/473-2377
Virginia	Caledon Natural Area *Guided eagle watching tours available*	40 - 50	June - September	Caledon Natural Area 540/663-3861
Washington	Skagit River Bald Eagle Natural Area	400	November - March	The Nature Conservancy 206/343-4344 Upper Skagit Bald Eagle Festival 360/853-7009
Wisconsin	Nelson Dewey State Park *Bald Eagle days in January*	200 - 300	December - March	Wisconsin Dept. Of Natural Resources 608/725-5374

Epilogue

*J*ack A. Barrie, America's foremost Bald Eagle photographer, was not able to see the completion of this book. On June 3, 1996, he called with devastating news: He had terminal cancer and was given only two months to live. Jack died in his wife's arms on August 1, 1996.

Jack's keen eyes brought images to life that no human eyes have seen before. Of the 20,000 photographs of Bald Eagles, this was his favorite.

"There was a wonderful stream of light that hit the eagle the moment I released the shutter," he said. "See the drops of water behind the eagle? They are like pearls from heaven!"

As the eagle flies skyward, we shall remember that life is fleeting and we all should be so lucky – as Jack – to seize life's special moments, and catch a few pearls from heaven.

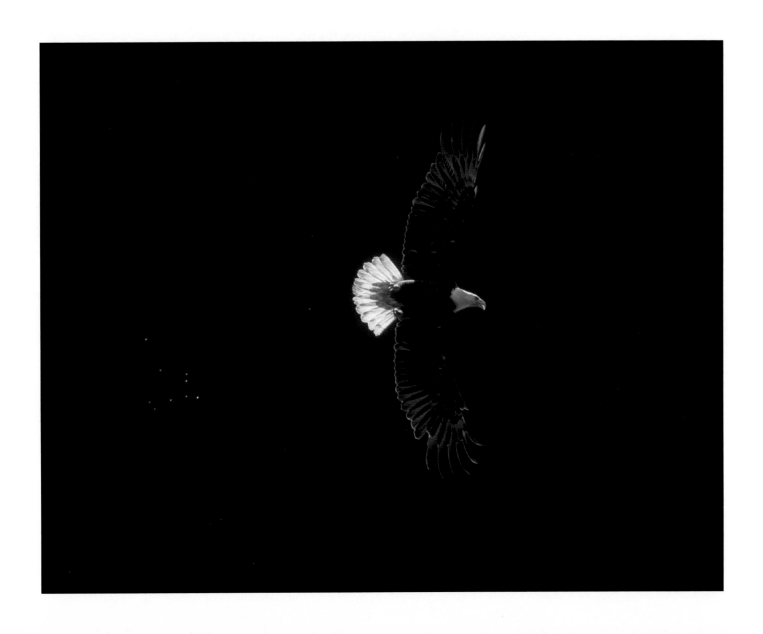

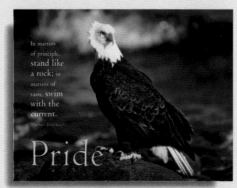